●= STEP-BY-STEP PROBLEM SOLVING

A Practical Guide
To Ensure Problems
Get (And Stay) Solved

Richard Y. Chang

P. Keith Kelly

Richard Chang Associates, Inc.
Publications Division
Irvine, California

STEP-BY-STEP
PROBLEM SOLVING

A Practical Guide To Ensure
Problems Get (And Stay) Solved

Richard Y. Chang
P. Keith Kelly

Library of Congress Catalog Card Number
93-77940

ISBN 1-883553-11-3

Third printing April 1994

Richard Chang Associates, Inc.
Publications Division
41 Corporate Park, Suite 230
Irvine, CA 92714
(800) 756-8096 • Fax (714) 756-0853

RICHARD
CHANG
ASSOCIATES

ACKNOWLEDGMENTS

About The Authors

Richard Y. Chang is President and CEO of Richard Chang Associates, Inc., a diversified organizational improvement consulting firm based in Irvine, California. He is internationally recognized and highly respected for his management strategy, quality improvement, organization development, customer satisfaction, and human resource development expertise.

P. Keith Kelly, a Senior Consultant at Richard Chang Associates, Inc., is an experienced educator, consultant, and management professional. His special areas of expertise encompass strategic planning and analysis, financial management, process improvement, and market research.

The authors would like to acknowledge the support of the entire team of professionals at Richard Chang Associates, Inc. for their contribution to the guidebook development process. In addition, special thanks are extended to the many client organizations who have helped us shape the practical ideas and proven methods shared in this guidebook.

Additional Credits

Editor:	Sarah Ortlieb Fraser
Reviewers:	Kevin Kehoe, Matt Niedzwiecki, and Ruth Stingley
Graphic Layout:	Christina Slater, Penelope Chaney, and Dottie Snyder
Cover Design:	John Odam Design Associates

PREFACE

The 1990's have already presented individuals and organizations with some very difficult challenges to face and overcome. So who will have the advantage as we move toward the year 2000 and beyond?

The advantage will belong to those with a commitment to continuous learning. Whether on an individual basis or as an entire organization, one key ingredient to building a continuous learning environment is *The Practical Guidebook Series*, brought to you by the Publications Division of Richard Chang Associates, Inc.

After understanding the future *"learning needs"* expressed by our clients and other potential customers, we are pleased to publish *The Practical Guidebook Series*. These guidebooks are designed to provide you, the reader, with proven *"real-world"* tips, tools, and techniques on a wide range of subjects which can be applied immediately in the workplace and/or on a personal level.

Once you've had a chance to benefit from *The Practical Guidebook Series*, please feel free to share your feedback with us. Your feedback is so important, we've even included a brief *Evaluation and Feedback Form* at the end of the guidebook which you may fax to us at (714) 756-0853.

With your feedback, we can continuously improve the resources we are providing through the Publications Division of Richard Chang Associates, Inc.

Wishing you successful reading,

Richard Y. Chang
President and CEO
Richard Chang Associates, Inc.

TABLE OF CONTENTS

"Within each problem lies a disguised opportunity . . . but it is the art of unmasking the disguise that distinguishes between the two."

Anonymous

"All problems become smaller if, instead of indulging them, you confront them. Touch a thistle timidly and it pricks you; grasp it boldly and its spine crumbles."

William S. Halsey

CHAPTER ONE

INTRODUCTION

Why Read This Guidebook?

Have you ever been in the position of tackling a problem only to stop and ask yourself or your team members, *"Didn't we solve this problem last year? What are we doing working on the same problem again?"* If this has happened to you, you know how frustrating it can be, putting time and effort into the same project over and over again.

And problems pop up whether you're on or off the job. Unfortunately, having good intentions doesn't always mean problems get solved. Things go wrong in the process. Underlying assumptions change. Perhaps your solution is only a quick fix, a temporary Band-Aid that doesn't solve the problem permanently.

This guidebook can help. It presents a time-tested approach to problem solving. The Six-Step Problem-Solving Model follows a logical path, starting with identifying a problem clearly and leading to a plan of action to solve it.

One of the purposes of this guidebook is to help you become more successful at problem solving by teaching you how to avoid the common problem-solving pitfalls. Examples of some of these pitfalls are presented in Appendix A. Take a few moments and read them before starting the rest of the book. Maybe you'll recognize yourself in one or more of these situations!

Who Should Read This Guidebook?

This guidebook is designed for individuals, and small groups working in problem-solving teams. Although the examples and scenarios that follow take place in a business setting, the concepts and methods of problem solving work in other settings, such as community and nonprofit organizations and even personal situations.

When And How To Use It

Use this material in a group, or on an individual basis, as a guide to solving problems in a systematic manner. This guidebook will train you to cover all the bases of problem solving, and it will help you ensure objectivity. Additionally, it can serve as a tool to help you successfully manage people in a problem-solving team.

When faced with a complicated or tough problem, it is useful to follow each step of the model in detail. When the problem is straightforward, breeze through certain steps and focus attention on the one or two steps that are most critical to the solution.

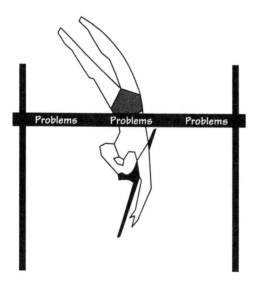

This problem-solving model isn't slick-sounding theory. It works! Like any set of abilities and techniques, from those of the professional athlete to those of a skilled technician, practice is the key to achieving the best results. By practicing the techniques that follow, you too can become successful at solving problems once and for all!

A variety of worksheets have been included at the ends of Chapters Five through Ten, which you may want to use to jot down notes, key ideas, and/or details of your own problem-solving efforts.

Each of the tools and techniques used in the Six-Step Problem-Solving Model are explained in more detail in Appendix B. Also included are blank worksheets labeled *"Reproducible Form,"* which you are encouraged to copy and use frequently.

In addition, several tools and techniques essential to successful problem solving, including Check Sheets, Control Charts, and Cause and Effect Diagrams, are mentioned. These tools are covered in detail in other guidebooks in the *Quality Improvement Series*. These guidebooks—entitled *Continuous Improvement Tools, Volumes 1 and 2*, also describe the use of other valuable methods that can help you become a more successful problem solver.

CHAPTER TWO

WHY A SYSTEMATIC PROBLEM-SOLVING MODEL?

Why have a model to follow when trying to solve problems? Why not simply agree on the solution and do what has to be done?

Perhaps General George S. Patton answered these questions best when he said:

> *"If you tell people where to go, but not how to get there, you'll be amazed at the results."*

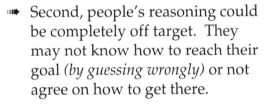

Patton's theory can be interpreted in two ways:

⟹ First, people are creative thinkers and would figure out a wonderful way to reach the destination on their own.

⟹ Second, people's reasoning could be completely off target. They may not know how to reach their goal *(by guessing wrongly)* or not agree on how to get there.

Indeed, starting off on the problem-solving path without a model to guide you to the desired destination may produce amazing results. Some of these results are outlined in the various pitfall examples in Appendix A. Using a systematic model will help you avoid these and other pitfalls.

CHAPTER THREE

THE SIX-STEP
PROBLEM-SOLVING MODEL

You may have experienced problem solving as a one-step process—
solve it. But there's more to it than that. For starters, you have to
know what the problem really is, what's causing it, and look at new
and creative ways of solving it. These areas are covered in the
following pages, providing a step-by-step model you can use in
your organization.

The problem-solving model can be used as a road map for you and
your team to follow. It will help you find the right solutions and
avoid some of the problem-solving pitfalls you may have
experienced in the past.

The model is set up to be followed one step at a
time, but you may not need to follow each step in
depth in every problem-solving situation. For
example, if your problem is already clearly
defined *(Step One)*, you can go straight to Step
Two. Or maybe the root causes are already
obvious *(Step Two)*, so you can breeze through
that step of analyzing the causes.

When you put the model into practice, you might get to a step and find you have to retrace your steps and start again. For example, you may begin analyzing causes and realize you should go back and define the real problem again.

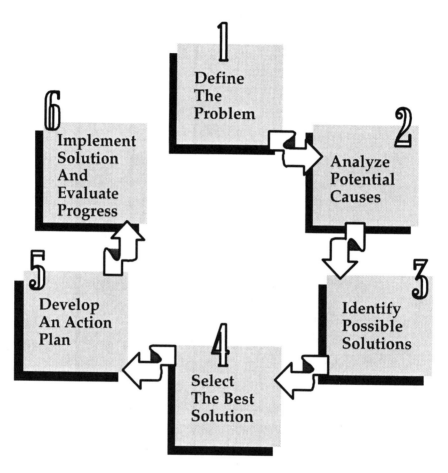

SIX–STEP PROBLEM–SOLVING MODEL

Using the problem-solving model will involve you in two *"expanding"* and two *"shrinking"* phases. The model goes from a starting point and expands to a long list of possible causes and solutions. At other times, the model shrinks these long lists down to a few key causes and solutions.

Why do this? Because we tend to limit ourselves and not look far enough to find answers. If you make it your goal to uncover several causes of your problem, you'll have a wider scope of information and more insight into the problem.

Following is a brief explanation of what takes place in each of the six problem-solving steps.

STEP	METHOD	DESCRIPTION
1. **Define The Problem**	DEFINITION Problem Statement: Desired State:	Write a concise statement of the existing problem, then briefly summarize where you want to be after the problem has been resolved.

STEP	METHOD	DESCRIPTION
2. **Analyze Potential Causes**	CAUSE AND EFFECT DIAGRAM	Identify the potential causes and determine the most likely root cause(s) of the problem.

STEP	METHOD	DESCRIPTION
3. **Identify Possible Solutions**	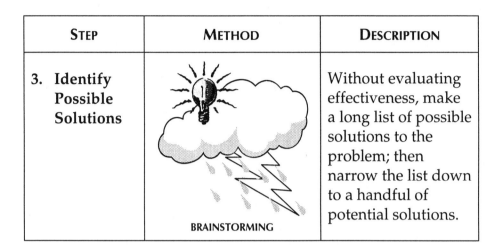 BRAINSTORMING	Without evaluating effectiveness, make a long list of possible solutions to the problem; then narrow the list down to a handful of potential solutions.

STEP	METHOD	DESCRIPTION
4. **Select The Best Solution**	**CRITERIA RATING FORM**	Evaluate possible solutions by rating each against three to six criteria. Choose the best of the group!

CRITERIA RATING FORM

Criteria	Solution	Solution	Solution
	X	X	X
		X	
		X	X

STEP	METHOD	DESCRIPTION
5. Develop An Action Plan	**ACTION PLAN** WHAT / WHO / WHEN	Write a detailed plan that lists action steps, responsible person(s), start/end dates, estimated hours, and cost.

STEP	METHOD	DESCRIPTION
6. Implement Solution And Evaluate Progress	**ACTION PLAN** WHAT / WHO / WHEN ✓ ✓ ✓ ✓	Follow up using the Action Plan to ensure the action steps are achieved!

Now let's take a look at a case example we will be using throughout the rest of the guidebook to demonstrate how the problem-solving model works.

CHAPTER FOUR

PROBLEM SOLVING
ONE STEP AT A TIME

Case Example: BTB Distribution, Inc.

BTB Distribution, Inc. *(BTB)* had a problem. When the management team reviewed the company's financial and operating results for the second quarter of the year, they discovered that the Customer Satisfaction Index figures were below target. In fact, for the second quarter in a row, the index had dropped, this time from 84 to 81 *(on a scale of 1 to 100)*.

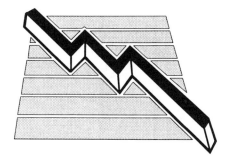

The figure had been flat or declining slightly during the past year. Management discussed the matter at the last quarterly meeting *(when the index had dropped from 86 to 84)*. Each Vice President agreed to look at the issue from his or her division's perspective.

Although each division spearheaded several discussions, the slide continued. Finally, management decided to take a systematic approach to dealing with the problem. They established a five-member cross-functional team, charged with analyzing the problem, coming up with the best possible solution(s), and recommending a plan to solve the problem.

The basis for choosing the team was different from BTB's usual approach, which involved putting a team of senior people together—all chosen because they had the authority and the understanding of *"the big picture."* It was assumed that they were the best qualified to handle the job.

This time, however, the team was made up of the people closest to the customers and the company's products and services. Management felt this would be an advantage in discovering what was going on and understanding how to solve it.

The team members selected were:

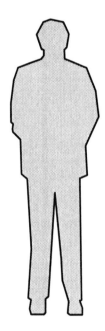

RON
Technical services manager
(and team leader)

MICHIYO
Technical support
representative

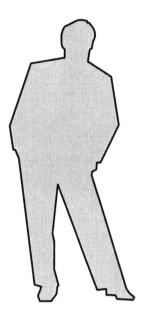

JOSÉ
Customer service
representative

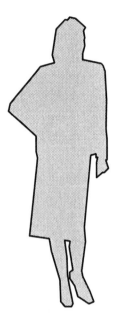

CYNTHIA
Customer service
representative

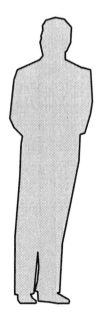

RENAUD
Marketing
representative

STEP ONE: DEFINE THE PROBLEM

"A problem well-defined is a problem half-solved."

Anonymous

The first step in successfully solving a problem is defining it in a way that it can be solved. There are two parts to successfully defining a problem:

A. Develop a problem statement

B. Identify a *"desired state"* or goal

Countless problem-solving efforts have gone offtrack because not enough attention was paid to this critical first step. With their problem clearly defined, a team can focus all of its energy in the same direction. On the other hand, if the problem is not well-defined, people will have different perceptions of what they are working on. As a result, they may come up with very different ideas of how to solve the problem.

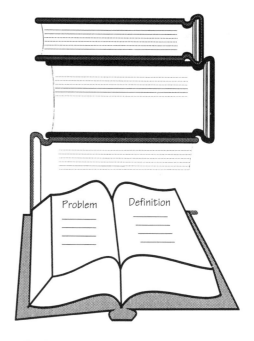

The best way to ensure that the problem is clearly understood by everyone involved is to actually define it in writing.

Here is how the BTB team defined the problem they were facing:

PROBLEM DEFINITION

The Problem Statement:

The Customer Satisfaction Index has declined from 89 to 81 in the last 12 months.

The Desired State:

The Customer Satisfaction Index will be at least 89 six months from now (by the end of the fourth quarter, 199X), and will not decline thereafter.

This was the result of much discussion; it was by no means the first attempt at defining the problem. Members of the team actually proposed and discussed several definitions of the problem before agreeing that this straightforward statement was the best starting point in tackling the problem.

Following is the process they went through, some of the other problem definitions they considered, and the pitfalls they managed to avoid in this critical first step.

Develop A Problem Statement

Develop a problem statement that accurately and clearly describes the current condition your team wants to change. Consider the following questions:

♦ **Is the problem stated objectively?** Is it stated in such a way that it doesn't slant the situation in favor of one approach or another, and doesn't leave room for interpretation? It should be a simple statement of fact.

♦ **Is the problem limited in scope?** The problem should be defined so that it is small enough for a team or individual to realistically tackle and solve.

♦ **Does everyone involved have a common understanding of the problem?** It should be written in such a way that everyone can understand it.

In summary, the problem statement should be objective, and written in clear, simple terms!

Here are a couple of hints for you to keep in mind when developing a problem statement:

⟶ Avoid including any *"implied cause"* in the problem statement

⟶ Avoid including any *"implied solution"* in the problem statement

This first point—to avoid including any *"implied cause"*—deals with the possibility that the problem statement might include a reference to a cause of your problem. If so, you might start working on the problem with that cause in mind—and what if that's not the main or only cause of the problem?

An example of an unproductive problem statement is BTB's first attempt:

 "Competitor advertising and our recent product problem have reduced customer satisfaction."

In this problem statement there are actually two *"implied causes,"* the advertising campaign and an undefined recent product problem. Although one or both of these may have something to do with the problem, they may not be the only causes, or the root of the problem. By choosing this statement as its problem statement, the BTB team could be headed in the wrong direction.

Product Problems Advertising

The second point—to avoid including *"implied solutions"* in a problem statement—will help steer problem solvers away from confusion as well. How can you possibly know the solution to a problem before you've grasped the problem itself and its cause(s)?

Two other unproductive problem statements the BTB team considered were:

"The product selection process needs to be revamped and streamlined."

and

"The advertising needs to focus on emphasizing how satisfied the majority of our customers are."

Both of these statements contain an *"implied solution."*

The obvious danger of beginning a problem–solving effort with an *"implied solution"* or an *"implied cause"* is that the team may not try to find out the true causes or explore all of the possible solutions.

The actual problem statement the team decided on describes the problem situation as objectively as possible, and how it currently exists:

"The Customer Satisfaction Index has declined from 89 to 81 during the last 12 months."

This problem statement is simple, clear, and does not include any implied causes or solutions. It is a statement of the problem the team needs to solve.

Once the problem is defined in clear and objective terms, your team can focus all of its energy in the same direction.

Identify A Desired State Or Goal

The *"desired state"* is where you want to be when the problem is solved. Once the BTB team had defined the problem, it was relatively easy to identify their desired state.

"The Customer Satisfaction Index will be at least 89 six months from now (by the end of the 4th quarter, 199X), and will not decline thereafter."

Defining the desired state, or goal, provides focus and direction. A measurable goal, as this example contains, makes it possible to track progress as the problem is being solved. It also makes evaluating the effectiveness of the solution easier!

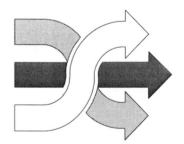

In this case, the team was concerned about getting pushed by management and others *(or even by themselves)* to come up with a *"quick fix"* to the problem. It may explain why the team members added *"and will not decline thereafter"* to the end of their statement. Their goal was to find a long-term solution to their problem.

Tests Of A Good Problem Statement

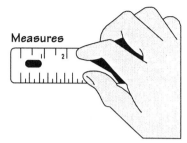

☞ Problem statement and desired state contain measures

☞ No *"implied causes"*

☞ No *"implied solutions"*

☞ *"Short and sweet"*—no more than 10 or 15 words if possible

☞ Can pass the *"So what?"* test

The BTB team's final problem statement passes these tests. You may be wondering what the *"So what?"* test is. Before putting in the time and effort on a problem-solving project, the definition stage requires that your team ask itself *"So what?"* in terms of the problem statement.

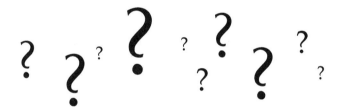

In other words, is the problem worth solving, and why? If a problem passes the *"So what?"* test, the members of a team or any individual working on the problem will prove to themselves and others that the problem is important enough to continue solving. If the problem-solving team does not ask itself the *"So what?"* question, the rest of the organization will!

The *"So what?"* question, directed at BTB's problem of dealing with the drop in the Customer Satisfaction Index measure, drew the following responses:

> *"Because the decline in the Customer Satisfaction Index leads to a loss in sales and market share."*

"Because this problem makes us lose money."

"Because our competitors will advertise that their Customer Satisfaction Index is now higher than ours, which will draw away more customers."

With answers like these, it was obvious to the BTB team that the problem was serious. The company would face difficult issues if the problem was not solved.

Note: Passing the *"So what?"* test should guarantee that a problem not only exists, but that it's worth solving. In BTB's case, the team had no trouble deciding the problem was real. The index drop from 89 to 81 clearly signaled that something was wrong.

Armed with a clear definition of the problem and an understanding of the rationale for solving it, the team was ready to tackle the next step—finding out what was causing it.

But what if BTB didn't have an index to point out the drop in customer satisfaction? Other signals might have popped up, such as a drop in market share, fewer return customers, and so on. Whatever the signals would have been for BTB, or whatever they might be for you, the key is putting together facts and figures that can help you get a handle on the extent of the problem.

You might have to gather data at this point to confirm the existence of the problem. Although this may seem like a lot of extra work, especially if the problem is obvious to you, the information and data gathered will help you get others to *"buy in"* to the definition of the problem. This preliminary data will also steer you in the right direction toward finding possible causes of your problem, which is the next step in the process.

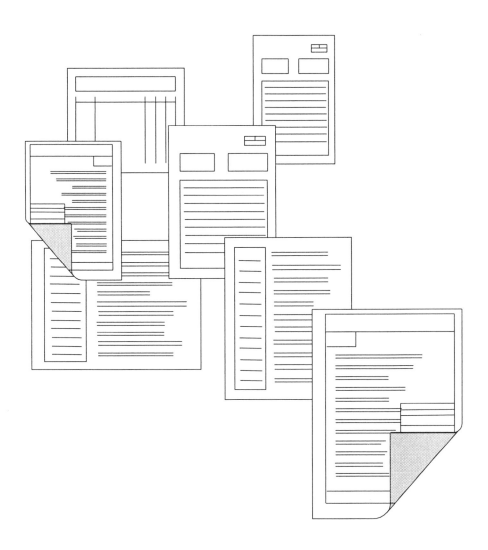

CHAPTER FIVE WORKSHEET:
DEFINING YOUR PROBLEM

Use this worksheet to complete Step One of the Six-Step Problem-Solving Model.

1. Write your problem statement in clear, concise, and specific terms.

_____

_____

_____

_____

_____

_____

Questions To Consider:

☐ Is the problem stated objectively and does it include *"just the facts"*?

☐ Is the scope of the problem limited enough for you and/or your team to handle?

☐ Will everyone who reads it have the same understanding of what the problem is?

☐ Does the problem statement include any *"implied causes"* or *"implied solutions"*?

2. Describe the *"desired state"*—the outcome you hope to reach by solving the problem.

_____

_____

_____

_____

_____

_____

_____

_____

_____

_____

Questions To Consider:

☐ Has the *"desired state"* been described in measurable terms?

☐ Have you included a target date?

☐ Will everyone be clear on whether this is considered a short-term or long-term *"desired state"*?

STEP TWO:
ANALYZE POTENTIAL CAUSES

"I keep six honest serving men
(They taught me all I know);
Their names are What and Why and When
And How and Where and Who."

Rudyard Kipling

Analyzing potential causes is the stage of problem solving where questions need to be asked and information needs to be gathered and sifted.

An easy trap to fall into is the one of assuming you know what is really causing a problem without taking the time and effort to dig deeper. This trap will hold you captive to analyzing symptoms, instead of freeing you to dig for the true root cause(s) of the problem you have defined.

Analyzing potential causes effectively is best accomplished by following these key sub-steps:

A.   Identify potential cause(s)

B.   Determine the most likely cause(s)

C.   Identify the true root cause(s)

As mentioned earlier, these sub-steps will expand as you list many potential causes, then shrink as you narrow down the list to a smaller group of *"most likely"* causes.

Let's take a look at how the BTB team used these three sub-steps to analyze the potential causes of their customer satisfaction problem.

Identify Potential Cause(s)

KEY POINTS	POSSIBLE METHODS
Identify all potential causes that are contributing to the problem. Develop a list of 20 to 30 of the most likely cause(s). You can use Cause and Effect Diagrams, as shown on the right, as well as Brainstorming, Force Field Diagrams, and other tools.	CAUSE AND EFFECT

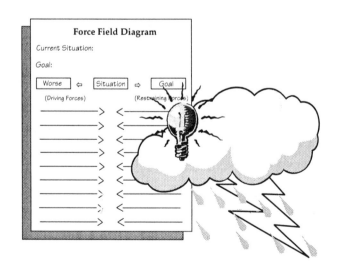

BTB's Cause and Effect Diagram

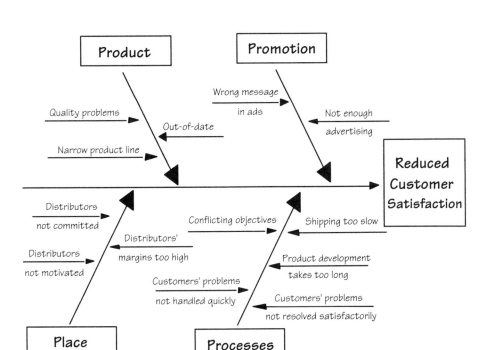

BTB's team members found the Cause and Effect Diagram (*also referred to as the fishbone, or Ishikawa diagram*) an effective means to uncovering potential causes of their problem.

Looking at BTB's diagram, you can see that the box at the end of the arrow lists the effect, or actual problem. All categories of potential causes lead off the straight line, or backbone, of the fishbone diagram.

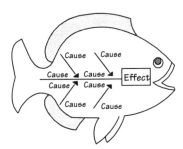

These potential causes can be categorized in various ways, such as Materials, Methods, Machines, and People (*the 3 M's and a P*), or Surroundings, Suppliers, Systems, and Skills (*the 4 S's*) and so on, depending on the type of situation.

In BTB's case, the effect was the problem of reduced customer satisfaction, and the causes were separated into the four categories of Product, Promotion, Place *(distribution structure)*, and Processes. If you are trying to decide whether to use the Cause and Effect Diagram or Brainstorming to identify potential causes of a problem, consider the following:

⟹ Brainstorming is most effective in producing a large quantity of ideas; but, because it is unstructured, additional work is required to categorize and organize the ideas once they are generated.

⟹ The Cause and Effect Diagram may not generate the quantity of ideas that Brainstorming does, but its more structured approach in using categories brings a team closer to clarifying the potential causes.

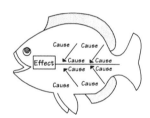

In some situations, such as in the case of broad company-wide problems, it may be better to brainstorm causes without the structure *(and perhaps constraints)* of a Cause and Effect Diagram. The problem-solving team can raise a wider range of possibilities, which will allow for more creative solutions.

The members of the BTB team also conducted a series of customer focus-group interviews to help them narrow down their long list of potential causes. This helped them identify the most likely causes of reduced customer satisfaction.

They also used the 80/20 rule *(also called the Pareto Rule)*, which states that *"80 percent of the effect can usually be attributed to 20 percent of the cause"* to help organize the most likely causes, which is the next step in the problem–solving process.

Determine The Most Likely Cause(s)

KEY POINTS	POSSIBLE METHODS
Use tools such as a Pareto Chart or team consensus to identify which are the most likely causes—those that contribute most to the problem.	 PARETO CHART

Look at the Pareto Chart. Note that the tallest bar, the one on the left, represents one cause, and the height of the bar, on a scale of zero to 100 percent, represents the percentage of the time that cause is considered critical to the problem. The second most critical cause is the next one to the right, and so on, with the last bar on the right usually representing all other causes lumped together.

BTB's Pareto Chart

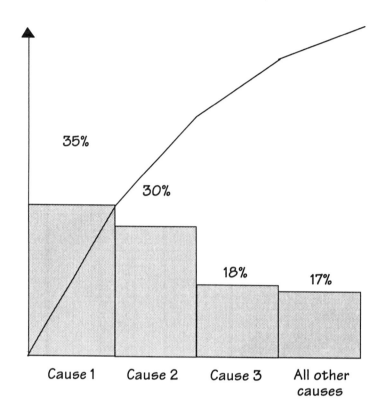

35%

30%

18%

17%

Cause 1   Cause 2   Cause 3   All other
causes

The focus-group interviews provided the members of the BTB team with figures that helped them rank the top three causes in order:

Cause # 1: Customer problems are not being resolved to their satisfaction *(35 percent).*

Cause # 2: Customer problems are not being handled quickly enough *(30 percent).*

Cause # 3: Customers are having product quality problems *(18 percent).*

From sixteen potential causes brainstormed by the team, these three causes were considered to be the most important source of customer dissatisfaction 83 percent of the time. The remaining thirteen causes accounted for only 17 percent of the problem.

The data and the way it was organized in the Pareto Chart brought the team to consensus on the most likely causes of the problem. The individuals who identified the major causes as pricing or competition issues were convinced to change their views. The Pareto Chart helped avoid the pitfall of focusing on areas that were easy to blame or areas in which team members had a particular interest or expertise.

The team decided to take the analysis to the next level, however, when they realized that the three most likely causes could be viewed as separate problems.

The members of the BTB team decided to subject each of the causes to its own analysis by digging for the underlying or root cause of each. Here is what they did.

Identify The True Root Cause(s)

KEY POINTS	POSSIBLE METHODS
Reanalyze the most likely causes to identify root causes by asking *"Why?"* several times. Another technique is to construct a flow chart of the work process behind the identified causes. This will help determine what's happening. A team can also treat the cause as a problem in itself and use the problem–solving model to solve it. You'll find it's not that difficult to ask and answer the *"Why?"* question five or six times.	**Successive Whys** 1. WHY? 2. WHY? 3. WHY? 4. WHY? 5. WHY?

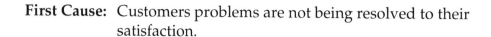

First Cause: Customers problems are not being resolved to their satisfaction.

WHY?

Because customer service contact personnel don't have the required technical information and support.

WHY?

Because customer support personnel have not been able to establish relationships with technical support people, and they do not receive continual training to keep abreast of product changes.

WHY?

Because many customer service contact personnel do not have the technical interests to build upon.

WHY?

Because the hiring criteria and training programs emphasized for customer service personnel in the last two years have shifted toward the people-skills side of customer service at the expense of technical skills and knowledge.

WHY?

Because the customer focus put in place in the organization over the last two years presented a strong focus on the people side of customer service. Management implemented the philosophy and approach so thoroughly they have lost sight of product-performance issues that are important to the customers.

Second Cause: Customer problems are not being handled quickly enough.

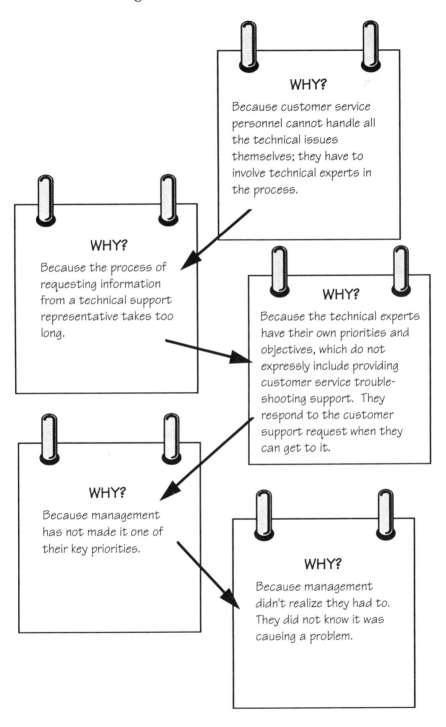

WHY?

Because customer service personnel cannot handle all the technical issues themselves; they have to involve technical experts in the process.

WHY?

Because the process of requesting information from a technical support representative takes too long.

WHY?

Because the technical experts have their own priorities and objectives, which do not expressly include providing customer service trouble-shooting support. They respond to the customer support request when they can get to it.

WHY?

Because management has not made it one of their key priorities.

WHY?

Because management didn't realize they had to. They did not know it was causing a problem.

Third Cause: Customers are having product quality problems.

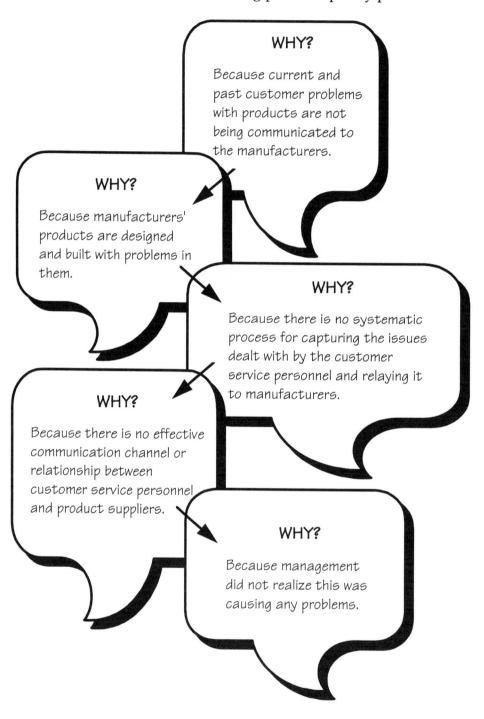

WHY?

Because current and past customer problems with products are not being communicated to the manufacturers.

WHY?

Because manufacturers' products are designed and built with problems in them.

WHY?

Because there is no systematic process for capturing the issues dealt with by the customer service personnel and relaying it to manufacturers.

WHY?

Because there is no effective communication channel or relationship between customer service personnel and product suppliers.

WHY?

Because management did not realize this was causing any problems.

The root causes of BTB's problem, derived from the repetitive *"Why?"* analyses, are:

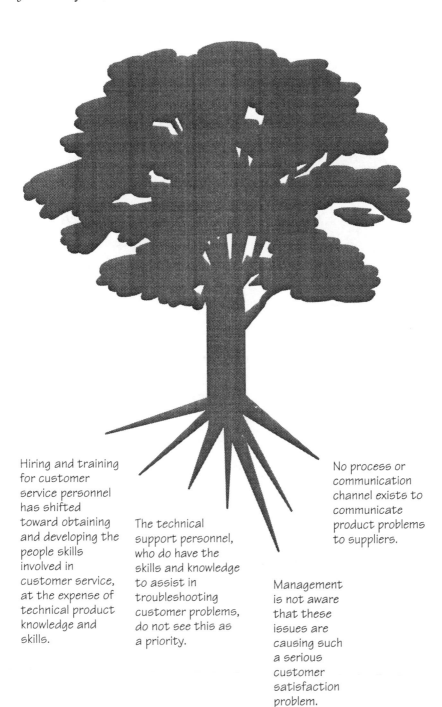

Hiring and training for customer service personnel has shifted toward obtaining and developing the people skills involved in customer service, at the expense of technical product knowledge and skills.

The technical support personnel, who do have the skills and knowledge to assist in troubleshooting customer problems, do not see this as a priority.

No process or communication channel exists to communicate product problems to suppliers.

Management is not aware that these issues are causing such a serious customer satisfaction problem.

At this stage in the Six-Step Problem-Solving Model, the problem has been clearly defined, and the causes have been identified *(using the Cause and Effect Diagram)*, prioritized *(using the Pareto Chart)*, and taken down to their root causes *(with the repetitive "Why?" analyses)*. You may need to put the brakes on at this point to make sure that these root causes are real and to what extent they exist.

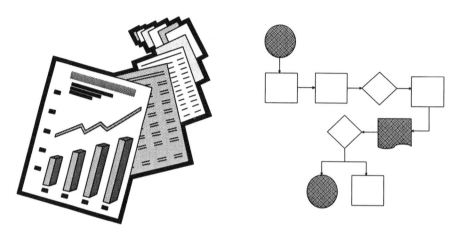

Depending on how large and involved the problem is, further analysis may be necessary, which can take the form of measurement, data gathering, interviews, observations of a process, or construction of a flow chart.

In BTB's case, the team was very confident about their choice of root causes. They were able to proceed directly to identifying possible solutions to the underlying root causes of the customer satisfaction problem.

CHAPTER SIX WORKSHEET:
ANALYZING POTENTIAL CAUSES

One of the key points made in this chapter is the need to look beyond the symptoms of a problem to get to the real *(or root)* causes. Use this worksheet as a tool in analyzing the potential causes of your problem.

1. Identify all potential causes of your problem.

> **Note:** See Appendix B for tips on using Brainstorming and the Cause and Effect Diagram. A Cause and Effect worksheet is included there for you to copy and use.

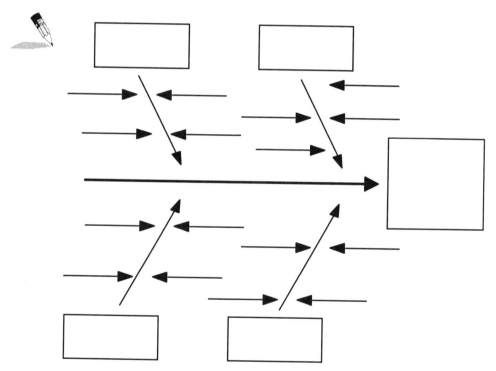

Questions To Consider:

☐ Have you explored all the potential causes?

☐ Did you get input from people closest to the problem?

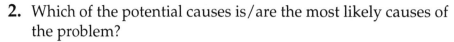

2. Which of the potential causes is/are the most likely causes of the problem?

Note: See Appendix B for tips on using Pareto Chart analysis. A Pareto Chart worksheet is included there for you to copy and use.

Your Observations

CAUSE	NUMBER OF TIMES CITED AS CAUSE	PERCENT OF TOTAL
(Cause)		
(Cause)		
(Cause)		
(Cause)		
(Cause) # n		
Total		**100%**

Your Pareto Chart

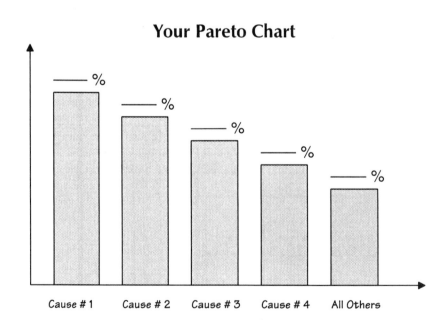

Questions To Consider:

❏ Are the most likely causes supported by your data?

❏ Will others agree with the selection of most likely causes, or will you be able to convince them?

3. What are the true root causes of the problem?

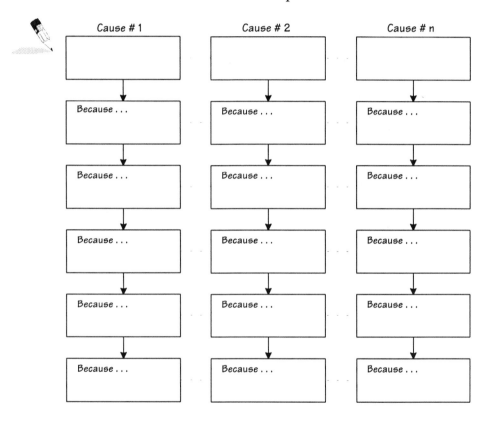

Questions To Consider:

❏ Did you ask *"Why?"* until you got to the real source(s) of the problem?

❏ Does your problem statement still hold as the best statement of the problem you are going to solve?

STEP THREE:
IDENTIFY POSSIBLE SOLUTIONS

"For there are few things as useless—if not as dangerous—as the right answer to the wrong question."

Peter E. Drucker, *The Practice of Management*

Once the causes of the problem have been identified to your satisfaction, it is important to generate ideas and alternatives *(even some wild ones)* for solving the problem. This is the stage in the problem–solving process that requires the maximum level of creativity.

For people faced with a problem within an organization, a natural reaction is to think about all the constraints, rules, and procedures that might narrow down the possible options for solving a problem. People's experience, what they think is acceptable to management, what has worked before, and all kinds of other boundaries restrict creativity when it comes down to the nitty-gritty of solving a problem.

Sometimes, the most creative and unexpected approach to the problem brings the best results. Being creative means putting ideas on the table that might sound farfetched at first.

For example, think about the person at Kodak who, not too long ago, approached management with the idea of making a camera so cheap and lightweight that people would throw it away after one use. It sounded like a crazy idea at first, but the results speak for themselves. Creativity pays off!

Identifying solutions is a two-part process:

A. Generate a list of possible solutions

B. Determine the best solutions

The first part of the process is to go for quantity with a broad list of possible solutions, while the second narrows the list down to a short list of the four to six best possible solutions.

Generating this broad list has a key advantage over the usual approach in many organizations, which is simply to come up with two or three alternative solutions from which to choose.

The downside of starting with a short list of alternatives is that one or more excellent solutions may be excluded from consideration. The two or three ideas listed may not be the top choices.

By starting out with a much longer list of possibilities, you improve your chances of exploring more innovative and unusual solutions, which would probably not be considered otherwise.

Let's take a look at how the members of the BTB team came up with their solutions and how they narrowed the list down to a manageable size. Your team will be able to use the same methods to uncover the best possible solutions to a problem.

Generate A List Of Possible Solutions

KEY POINTS	POSSIBLE METHODS
It's important to not stop too quickly in this process, since the first few ideas, or the most obvious ones, are not always the best. You can uncover potential solutions by comparing the problem to a similar problem you've solved before. ☞ Did you avoid passing judgment or making comments on possible solutions as they were raised? ☞ Did you *"think outside"* your own experience and expertise? ☞ Do you fully understand each possible solution? ☞ Did you go for quantity—at least 20 or so possible solutions?	 **BRAINSTORMING**

Here is the list the BTB team produced by using Brainstorming:

* Train customer service personnel
* Have technicians do customer service jobs one day a week
* Put both groups in the same department
* Have customer service personnel handle problems of minimal technical complexity only, then bring in technical support
* Set up a special hot line from customer service to technical support
* Rewrite job descriptions for customer service personnel to include need for technical knowledge
* Contract out the customer service troubleshooting function
* Have two or three technical experts physically work in the customer service area at all times
* Create "partner teams" of customer service and technical personnel
* Have managers work in customer service jobs to sensitize them to issues
* Incorporate negative customer feedback into product development process flow chart
* Revise written objectives of technical support personnel to include the priority objective of troubleshooting customer problems
* Hire new customer service personnel with required technical knowledge
* Conduct more testing of products before they are released
* Conduct technical knowledge testing of customer service personnel on a regular basis

Just as the members of the BTB team had to narrow their long list of causes, they also had to narrow their long list of potential solutions to a shorter, more workable list.

They used the Pareto Chart to narrow the long list of causes.
However, the BTB team used the following different approach to
choose their list of the five best possible solutions.

Determine The Best Solutions

KEY POINTS	POSSIBLE METHODS
Reduce the long list of possible solutions to the four to six best possible solutions. This can be done by using a Paired-Choice Matrix like the one on the right. To use it, begin with the first row *(Solution A)* and proceed across the row deciding which solution is the *best* solution between each pair. For example, you would first skip the choice between Solution A and Solution A, then choose between A and B, writing in the box your choice between the two. Continue across the row, making a choice between A and C, A and D, and so on.	

	Sol. A	Sol. B	Sol. C	Sol. D
Sol. A				
Sol. B				
Sol. C				
Sol. D				

PAIRED-CHOICE MATRIX

Repeat the process for each row until you have compared each possible pair. Then tally up the number of A's, B's, C's, etc. The solution(s) which you have chosen most frequently will become your short list.

The BTB team members narrowed their initial solution list down to the following short list.

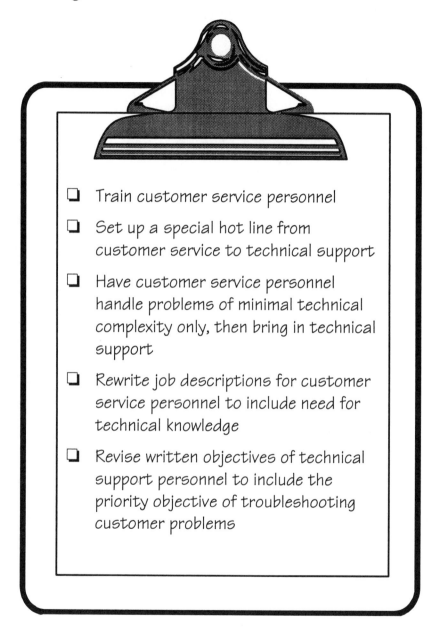

❏ Train customer service personnel

❏ Set up a special hot line from customer service to technical support

❏ Have customer service personnel handle problems of minimal technical complexity only, then bring in technical support

❏ Rewrite job descriptions for customer service personnel to include need for technical knowledge

❏ Revise written objectives of technical support personnel to include the priority objective of troubleshooting customer problems

The BTB team members were ready to proceed to Step Four, where they would select the best solution.

CHAPTER SEVEN WORKSHEET: IDENTIFYING POSSIBLE SOLUTIONS

Use this worksheet to identify solutions to a problem you have analyzed.

1. Generate a list of possible solutions.

    Note: See Appendix B for tips on using Brainstorming.

_____

Questions To Consider:

☐ Did you hold back from evaluating these proposed solutions?

☐ Did you make a point of *"thinking outside"* your own experience and expertise?

☐ Did you involve others in the process—especially those who have an interest in getting the problem solved?

2. Determine the best solutions from the brainstormed list.

	Solution A	Solution B	Solution C	Solution D	Solution N	Score by row
Solution A						
Solution B						
Solution C						
Solution D						
Solution N						

Questions To Consider:

❏ Did you narrow the list down to four to six possible solutions?

❏ Do you fully understand each of them?

❏ Do any of them need to be combined?

STEP FOUR:
SELECT THE BEST SOLUTION

"I now believe I have found the true solution."

Albert Einstein, 1925

So far, the BTB team has used the Six-Step Problem-Solving Model to define the problem, analyze the causes of the problem, and generate a list of possible solutions.

During Step Four, a decision has to be made—which solution(s) to choose. As with any decision, several factors enter into the process.

In many problem–solving situations, the different factors, or criteria, that individuals use to make their decisions, are unclear or never voiced. This can and does lead to misunderstandings and misinterpretations of other people's motives.

The following sub-steps will help ensure that you and your team reach an agreement and select the best solution(s) for your problem.

A. Develop and assign weights to criteria

B. Apply the criteria

C. Choose the best solution(s)

The BTB team of Ron, Michiyo, José, Cynthia, and Renaud have the job of deciding which of the five different alternatives is *(are)* the best long-term solution(s) to the BTB's customer satisfaction problem. While Ron may strongly favor Solution A, he may be focusing on one criterion only, such as low cost, for example.

Michiyo, on the other hand, may feel just as strongly about Solution D. Her choice, however, is the result of her criterion—to choose a solution that would meet the least resistance.

There are two keys to avoiding this possible deadlock.

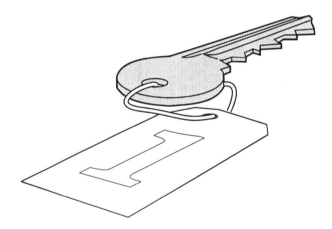

The first key is to put all the criteria people are thinking about out in the open and on the table. At this point, members are not yet clear on what criteria the others are using.

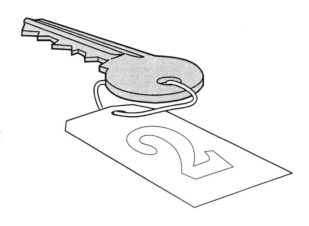

The second key is for the team to agree on how important these criteria are in relation to each other. The team should consider whether cost is the most important criterion, or whether low resistance by others should head the list, and so on. All criteria should be rated in terms of importance.

Here is how the BTB team handled the process:

Develop And Assign Weights To Criteria

KEY POINTS	POSSIBLE METHOD
Determine which criteria *(three to six)* are appropriate for selecting a solution to the problem. Make sure that you clearly define each criterion so that everyone has the same definition in mind. Apply weightings to the criteria to show how important they are relative to each other. *(This can be done by assigning a number to each criterion so that all the criteria together total 100.)*	BRAINSTORMING

BTB TEAM'S CRITERIA	DEFINED AS . . .	WEIGHT
Ease of implementation	How easy would it be to implement the solution?	20%
Probability of success	How likely is it that the solution itself could be successfully implemented?	20%
Effectiveness of solution	How effective would the solution be in addressing root causes and solving the problem?	50%
Relatively low resistance	How much resistance might there be to implementing this solution?	10%
	Total weighting	**100%**

Apply The Criteria

KEY POINTS	POSSIBLE METHOD
Rate each possible solution on your short list against the criteria. You can do this by giving a score (*on a scale of 1 to 10, for example*) to each solution for the first criteria, then moving down and repeating this process for each criterion. After a score has been assigned to each box, multiply the score by the weighting. Then add up the weighted scores for each solution. Your team may find it helpful to alternate the use of open discussion and specific methods (*such as voting*) in working through the selection process. Weighting the criteria helps you choose the best solution(s).	**CRITERIA RATING FORM** | Criteria	Solution	Solution	Solution
---	---	---	---
Criteria	X	X	X
Criteria		X	
Criteria		X	X	

The BTB team used a Criteria Rating Form to apply their criteria to the five solutions they were evaluating. As they discovered, a Criteria Rating Form is a very effective tool in coming to a consensus, because it compares alternatives objectively.

It also helps ensure that someone's favorite criterion is not overriding that of others in terms of importance, and guarantees equal consideration for alternative solutions.

Here is the Criteria Rating Form created by the BTB team.

		RATING SCALE: 1 TO 10				
		ALTERNATIVE SOLUTIONS				
		A. Train customer service personnel	**B.** Special hot line from customer service to technical support	**C.** Customer service personnel handle problems of minimal technical complexity only, then bring in technical support	**D.** Rewrite job descriptions for customer service personnel to include need for technical knowledge	**E.** Revise written objectives of technical support personnel to include the priority objective of trouble-shooting customer problems
CRITERIA	**WEIGHT**					
Ease of implementation (How easy would it be to implement this solution?)	20%	7 (1.4)	6 (1.2)	5 (1.0)	8 (1.6)	8 (1.6)
Probability of success (How likely is it that the solution itself could be successfully implemented?)	20%	8 (1.6)	7 (1.4)	7 (1.4)	10 (2.0)	10 (2.0)
Effectiveness of solution (How effective would the solution be in addressing root causes and solving the problem?)	50%	7 (3.5)	7 (3.5)	5 (2.5)	3 (1.5)	4 (2.0)
Relatively low resistance (How much resistance might there be to implementing this solution?)	10%	8 (0.8)	7 (0.7)	6 (0.6)	8 (0.8)	5 (0.5)
TOTAL POINTS	100%	7.3	6.8	5.5	5.9	6.1

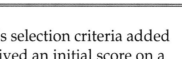
Note that the weighting of the BTB team's selection criteria added up to 100 percent, and each solution received an initial score on a scale of 1 to 10. The initial scores were then multiplied by the weights to come up with a weighted score for each box in the matrix.

The weighted scores for each solution were then tallied. As you can see, the total weighted scores range from a low of 5.5 for Solution C to a high of 7.3 for Solution A.

Take a moment to compare how the totals would have come out without weighting the criteria. The totals would have been:

Solution	Weighted Ranking	Unweighted Ranking
A	1	1
B	2	3
C	3	5
D	4	2
E	5	4

Although Solution A still has the highest score, whether or not the criteria was weighted, Solution D would have been second without the weightings, with a total of 29, as opposed to being the second-to-last choice (6.9) with the weightings.

You can see how things can turn out differently when you assign a weighting to the criteria. Try it in your next problem-solving situation, and you'll see how it makes it easier to come to an agreement on the *right* solution.

Choose The Best Solution(s)

KEY POINTS	POSSIBLE METHOD
Once all possible solutions have been evaluated against the identified criteria, choose the best solution(s) to be implemented. ⭲ Can the chosen solution(s) be realistically implemented?	

Out of the BTB team's five best solutions, the two with the highest score were:

SOLUTION	SCORE
⭲ Training the customer service personnel	7.3
⭲ Setting up a hot line between customer service and the technical personnel	6.8

The team agreed these solutions made sense. They were also confident that the process they went through gave them enough rationale for their conclusion. There would be no problem convincing the management team they had come up with the right course of action.

Just because the right solutions have been identified, however, it doesn't mean your task is completed. Now comes the tough part, turning the solutions into reality by following through and actually solving the problem.

This next step requires much work, involves many people, emphasizes planning, and so on. In the next chapter, we'll look at how a model for an Action Plan naturally follows the first four steps of the Six-Step Problem-Solving Model.

CHAPTER EIGHT WORKSHEET: SELECTING THE BEST SOLUTIONS

This worksheet will help you decide which solution(s) to select to solve your problem.

1. Which criteria *(four to six)* do you need to consider in selecting the best solution(s) to your problem?

    Note: See Appendix B for tips on using Brainstorming.

    _____

    _____

    _____

    _____

    _____

    _____

    _____

    _____

Questions To Consider:

❒ Are these criteria equally important?

❒ Will everyone involved have the same understanding of what each criterion means?

❒ Should you weight the criteria to reflect their importance *(total weights should equal 1 or 100 percent)*?

2. Apply the criteria to each of the solutions in your list of four to six.

Note: See Appendix B for tips on using Criteria Rating.

		RATING SCALE: 1 TO 10				
		ALTERNATIVE SOLUTIONS				
		A.	B.	C.	D.	E.
CRITERIA	WEIGHT					
TOTAL POINTS	100%					

Questions To Consider:

☐ Did you multiply the scores for each solution by the weighting for each criterion?

☐ Do the total weighted scores for each solution seem logical when you compare them with each other?

3. Choose the best solution.

_____

_____

_____

_____

Questions To Consider:

☐ Did you choose the solution with the highest score?

☐ Will you be able to persuade others this is the right choice?

_____

_____

_____

_____

STEP FIVE:
DEVELOP AN ACTION PLAN

The problem has only been solved on paper at this point; now it's time to get down to action. But what action? Where do you start? Who is going to do what, when, and how?

The following two sub-steps will help you address these questions and develop your Action Plan.

A. Divide the solution into sequential tasks

B. Develop contingency plans

Let's take a look at these sub-steps in more detail and see how the BTB team developed their Action Plan.

Divide The Solution Into Sequential Tasks

KEY POINTS	POSSIBLE METHODS
➠ Note responsible person(s) ➠ Schedule *(target dates)* for starting and completing Address the following questions: ➠ Have you considered those who will be affected by the implementation? ➠ Have you considered how you will implement the solutions? ➠ Have you considered what resources will be needed for the person to get his/her assigned task completed *(e.g., people, money, equipment, information, etc.)*? ➠ Have you considered the need for information and results to be shared, *(among tasks and activities that are directly related to each other)*?	**ACTION PLAN** <table><tr><th>What</th><th>Who</th><th>When</th></tr><tr><td>Design</td><td>John</td><td>8/24</td></tr><tr><td>Test</td><td>John</td><td>9/6</td></tr><tr><td>Proof</td><td>Gayle</td><td>9/17</td></tr><tr><td>Revise</td><td>Mary</td><td>10/8</td></tr><tr><td>Deliver</td><td>Gayle</td><td>11/1</td></tr></table>

Here is the Action Plan the BTB problem-solving team developed.

ACTION PLAN					
Action Step Task/Activity	**Responsible Person/ Group**	**Begin Date**	**End Date**	**Estimated Hours**	**Cost**[1]
Present solutions, Action Plan, and background to management team for go-ahead	Ron to lead All play a role	4/20	4/21	16	$480
Revise (if necessary) and finalize Action Plan	Ron	4/22	4/23	2	$60
Solution A: Training Customer Service personnel					
• Develop questionnaire and survey Customer Service personnel to determine current skill levels and gaps	Renaud and Michiyo (support from Personnel)	5/3	5/15	30	$900

ACTION PLAN (Page 2)					
Action Step Task/Activity	Responsible Person/ Group	Begin Date	End Date	Estimated Hours	Cost[1]
• Survey technical support personnel to find most frequently asked customer questions/ problems	José and Cynthia	5/3	5/15	20	$600
• Design training program	Renaud, Cynthia, and Personnel	5/21	6/25	200	$6,000
• Conduct training	Ron and Personnel	7/1	8/10	20-40 (from project team tracking progress)	$600 to $1,200
Solution B: Establish hot line from Customer Service to Technical Support					
• Communicate goal and plan to both groups— get input on how to proceed	Ron and José	5/4	5/12	8	$240

ACTION PLAN (Page 3)					
Action Step Task/Activity	Responsible Person/ Group	Begin Date	End Date	Estimated Hours	Cost[1]
• Check hardware and software alternatives and cost	Ron and José (support from Facilities Management)	5/6	5/14	6	$180
• Acquire and install system	Ron, Facilities Management, and vendor	5/20	6/16	10	$300 (System cost = $2,000 to $5,000)
• Train and test	Personnel and vendor	6/18	6/26	10 (project team tracking progress)	$300
• Check new Customer Satisfaction Index numbers and plan further improvements	All	7/15	7/20	20	$600
			TOTALS	342 to 382	$12,260 to $15,860

[1]Costs for the expected time to be spent by the problem–solving team members are included. We used $30 per hour which includes fringe benefits. The time for other groups, such as Personnel and Facilities Management, has not been included (since the Action Plan is being used mainly to plan the activities and time for the team itself).

Note that the BTB team members factored in an important step at the end of their Action Plan. Once their two solutions are well underway, they plan to look at further improvements. At that point, they may decide to implement one or more of the other solutions they previously identified, or they may choose some other path. Their decision will be based on the results of their Action Plan.

Tied in with your Action Plan should be a contingency plan, just in case. Why should you have a contingency plan? Have you ever had an experience in which even the best of plans got stalled, sidetracked, or had to be changed midstream, because of something that came up along the way?

Develop Contingency Plans

KEY POINTS	POSSIBLE METHODS
Points to consider: ⇒ What specific opportunities and threats may occur? ⇒ How will we deal with those opportunities and threats? ⇒ What can be done to prevent those potential problems from occurring?	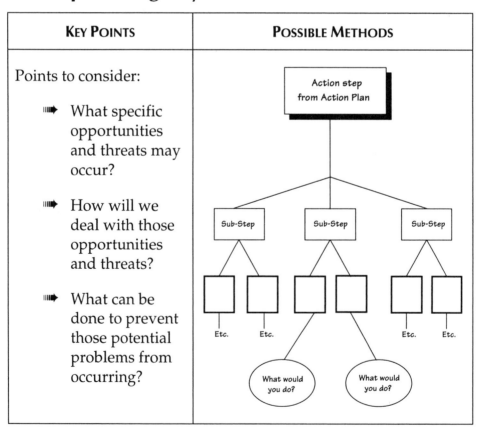

While you certainly can't stop the unexpected from happening, you can prepare for potential kinks in your operation by having a contingency plan. With a contingency plan on the back burner, you can keep your momentum going, instead of having to stop and figure out what to do when the unplanned events occur.

The BTB team members devised a few contingency plans to cover the potential difficulties they could anticipate. Following is an example of one contingency plan Renaud and Michiyo designed to handle potential threats to developing a questionnaire.

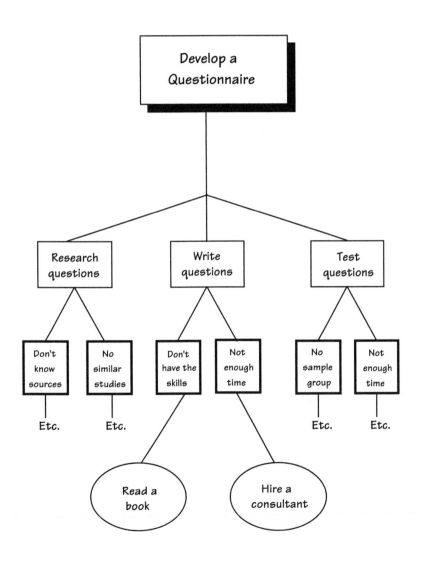

CHAPTER NINE WORKSHEET:
DEVELOPING YOUR ACTION PLAN

This worksheet will help you develop your Action Plan to implement the chosen solution(s) to your problem.

1. What tasks or activities need to be carried out to implement the solution? Who will be responsible for each and what are the target dates for completion?

   Note: See Appendix B for tips on using Action Plans. An Action Plan worksheet is included there for you to copy and use.

ACTION PLAN					
Action Step Task/Activity	Responsible Person/ Group	Begin Date	End Date	Estimated Hours	Cost[1]
				TOTALS		

Questions To Consider:

❏   Have you considered those who will be affected?

❏   Have you considered the resources that will be needed?

❏   Have you considered how information will be shared?

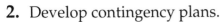

2. Develop contingency plans.

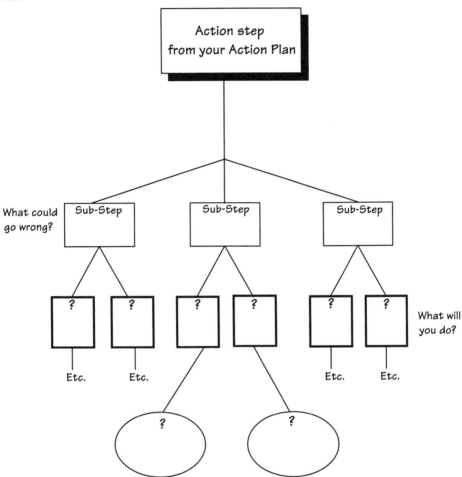

Questions To Consider:

☐ Have you focused on developing contingency plans for the most critical Action Steps?

☐ Are the necessary people aware of the contingency plan?

STEP SIX:
IMPLEMENT SOLUTION AND
EVALUATE PROGRESS

You should be prepared to modify your Action Plan, as necessary, to account for unexpected events. It is this step of the problem-solving process that makes the structured approach a *"closed loop."* The importance of the *"closed loop"* approach to solving problems becomes evident when you realize that circumstances, situations, people, and preferences change over time. By tracking the implementation of the Action Plan and evaluating progress, you can ensure the solutions are implemented even with those types of changes.

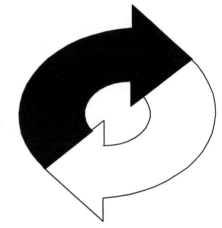

The following three sub-steps will make this stage of problem solving work successfully for you.

  A. **Collect data according to the Action Plan**

  B. **Implement contingency plans**

  C. **Evaluate results**

The BTB team stayed together to implement the problem. Ron's role of leading the team through the process of defining, analyzing, and coming up with solutions to the problem changed to one of managing the implementation and the Action Plan. Let's take a look at how they handled implementing their Action Plan and evaluating their progress.

Collect Data According To The Action Plan

KEY POINTS	POSSIBLE METHODS
Through an established monitoring system, determine whether or not specific tasks are being performed or short-term targets are being achieved as planned. Identified milestones and the control system associated with monitoring targets should be tracked and updated regularly.	INTERVIEWING 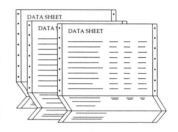 DATA SHEETS

Ron first clarified his expectations of the team members and made sure all members understood their responsibilities and accountabilities. He scheduled regular team meetings to review progress and deal with any obstacles faced by team members. He had team members keep him up-to-date practically every day on issues affecting whether they were able to meet the dates stated in the Action Plan.

Implement Contingency Plans

KEY POINTS	POSSIBLE METHODS
As conditions change during the monitoring and evaluation of Action Plans, implement necessary contingency plans to continue moving you toward the *"desired state."*	**ACTION PLAN** | What	Who	When
---	---	---
Design	John	8/24
Test	John	9/6
Proof	Gayle	9/17
Revise	Mary	10/8
Deliver	Gayle	11/1	 Driving Forces → [Current Situation] ← Restraining Forces **FORCE FIELD DIAGRAM**

Fortunately, the BTB team members didn't have to utilize any of their contingency plans, because everything went just about according to the Action Plan they had set up.

Evaluate Results

KEY POINTS	POSSIBLE METHODS
Repeat the six-step process to address additional problems as needed. ⇒ Has the *"desired state"* been accomplished? ⇒ Are plans in place to ensure that the problem will not recur?	**BRAINSTORMING** **DEFINE THE PROBLEM**

The team members checked the customer satisfaction numbers for the quarter ending in June and were very pleased to find that the slide had stopped. The index had moved up from 81 to 82 already, even though the solutions had only just been implemented.

CHAPTER TEN WORKSHEET:
IMPLEMENTING YOUR SOLUTION AND
EVALUATION PROGRAM

Use this worksheet to determine the approach you will use to implement the solution(s) and evaluate progress.

1. What data will you collect to ensure the action steps have been completed? How will you collect it?

_____

_____

_____

_____

_____

_____

_____

_____

_____

Questions To Consider:

❑ What role will others play in evaluating progress during implementation?

❑ How will you know if the implementation is offtrack?

2. What is your approach to implementing contingency plans?

_____

_____

_____

_____

Questions To Consider:

❏ How will you know when to implement a contingency plan?

❏ Who makes the decision?

❏ How will it be communicated?

3. Evaluate the results of your solution and identify new problems that might arise.

_____

_____

_____

_____

Questions To Consider:

❏ Has the desired state been reached?

❏ Are plans in place to ensure the problem does not recur?

CHAPTER ELEVEN

SUMMARY

With hindsight, you can probably think of instances in your organization where the Six-Step Problem-Solving Model would have produced better solutions to problems. Maybe you can even identify which of the steps would have been the most critical to arriving at the right solutions.

Often, problem definition is the key. If the problem is not clearly defined, all the good intentions and committed efforts that follow won't guarantee that you'll find the right solutions, let alone implement them!

Another pitfall that can short-circuit the process is jumping to conclusions—going straight to solutions without determining the real cause of the problem. Using the tools introduced in this guidebook can help you and your team avoid this pitfall and get to the root of the problem.

Coming up with creative solutions and using a tool such as the Criteria Rating Form to decide which solution(s) will solve the problem are also critical stages in successful problem solving.

And, of course, having an Action Plan and evaluating progress ensures that you close the loop and your ideas become reality.

May all your future problem-solving efforts be successful!

COMMON
PROBLEM-SOLVING PITFALLS

Solving problems is something we all do as part of our regular
daily activities, whether on-the-job or outside of work.

Problem solving can be challenging and frustrating at the same
time. The challenges arise when we have opportunities to take on a
problem that interests us and we can use our creative skills to come
up with solid, lasting solutions.

On the other hand, there are many pitfalls on the path to successful
problem solving that can lead to frustration and can knock your
problem-solving efforts offtrack.

Following are some of these pitfalls, which you will avoid by using
the proven Six-Step Problem-Solving Model.

PITFALL # 1

Working On Problems That Are Too General, Too Large, Or Not Well-Defined

This pitfall could also be described as the organizational equivalent of trying to solve the problem of world hunger. Biting off too large of a problem can lead to frustration, confusion, loss of momentum, and less motivation on the part of the individual or team working on the problem.

In the case of a large kitchenware manufacturer faced with tough competition, the company felt its problem was its production costs. For several years, the company focused its attention on what seemed to be the obvious solution—reducing production costs. Costs did go down, but the company's profitability and market share did not improve.

The company's sales force pushed the products that sold the easiest—those with the lowest price. As a result, the company had been selling more and more of the less profitable lines, which the competitors were not that interested in anyway.

And the more the company reduced its production costs, the more it ended up cutting its price, which put more pressure on cutting production costs. Finally, the company slammed on the brakes and redefined the problem. Things took a turn for the better after the company defined the problem as not having a profitable mix of products in its product line. By correctly defining the problem, they were able to successfully solve it.

PITFALL # 2

Jumping To A Solution Before Really Analyzing The Problem

This can happen when you are under the gun with pressing deadlines. You focus more on getting to a solution than figuring out if it is the *right* solution, one that will really solve the problem.

In one company, this misplaced focus led management to upgrade their computer system again and again, because every few months the computer wasn't fast enough and didn't have enough memory to keep up with work demands.

After the company *"solved"* this problem with the same solution for the fourth time in less than two years, one of the programmers suggested they take a deeper look at the problem. The reason the system kept running out of memory and slowing down was that two software bugs *(that nobody knew about)* automatically made copies of the files in memory.

The right solution was to fix the bugs *(root cause)*, instead of spending more and more money on extra equipment. This solved the problem once and for all. Up to this point, the company had been dealing with symptoms of the problem. Once the employees found the real cause of the problem, the rest was easy.

PITFALL # 3

Failing To Involve Critical Decision Makers
Or Employees Affected By The Problem
When Identifying Potential Solutions

Someone once coined the expression, *"Each of you in this company is the CEO of your own work area."* The message is that the people closest to where the work gets done know the most about what the problems are and what needs to be done to fix them. The employees affected by the problem need to be directly involved in the problem-solving process.

A small service company recently discovered that incoming phone calls from prospective customers were being routed seemingly at random by the primary and back-up receptionists. A group of four of the more experienced employees who should have been receiving the bulk of the calls began to propose solutions to the problem. They spent several hours in meetings weighing the pros and cons of the different solutions before finally agreeing on a *(compromise)* solution.

When the solution was presented to the receptionists, though, the response was, *"Oh that won't work because … Why don't we just do this?"* As it turned out, the receptionists' solution made more sense. If the affected employees *(the receptionists)* had been involved in the first place, the team could have saved themselves several hours, and the *right* solution could have been implemented quickly and effectively.

PITFALL # 4

Tackling Problems That Are Beyond The Control Or Influence Of The Individual Or Team

This can happen when individuals or members of a team begin to work on a problem situation in which they can't influence the outcome by themselves *(e.g., they may not be able to effectively carry out the Action Plan themselves, effectively influence others to do it, etc.)*.

In one example of this pitfall, Larry, a new assistant plant manager, wanted to solve what he felt were problems in the plant's warehousing operations. The previous assistant plant manager had let the warehouse employees work out their own problems. Larry went ahead and presented his solutions to the warehouse supervisor to implement, without consulting her employees up-front. Needless to say, Larry had a tough time getting the warehouse employees to agree with his solution.

The lesson here is that since Larry did not have the ability to influence or control the problem himself, he should have involved the warehouse supervisor and her employees, instead of trying to tackle the problem on his own.

PITFALL # 5

Applying "Pet" Solutions Rather Than Seeking A Creative Solution

This pitfall can be compared to the *"ugly baby syndrome"*—in which case someone has a predetermined idea about what the best solution *(their baby)* is and nobody else can criticize it.

The owner of a tour–boat company recently provided a great example of this pitfall. He had a pet solution for just about any problem that came up in his company, which was to blame someone or something outside of the company's control.

In one instance, the company was experiencing problems with the propellers on its newest boat, and in a high-profile excursion with local bigwigs aboard, the boat broke down and had to be towed back to the dock for repairs.

The owner immediately blamed the engine supplier who had fitted the engines and propellers; and, although some of the company's managers and captains suspected the problem might be closer to home, they went along with the owner and seriously criticized the supplier as well.

PITFALL # 5

(continued)

The owner had his attorney file a claim against the supplier, and the matter went to court. As it turned out, the new engines and shafts required a different type of lubricant than the older boats *(which the supplier had pointed out and supplied to the tour-boat company)*. However, the company had not followed the new procedure, and, somewhat embarrassed, realized that they, not the supplier, were the cause of the problem.

The owner finally realized he should not jump to conclusions and push his solutions on his team, who had good ideas, insights, and contributions of their own to make to a problem-solving process.

PITFALL # 6

Failing To Develop Good
Reasons For Choosing A Solution

Sometimes a solution will be chosen for the wrong reason(s). The rationale for choosing one of three possible solutions, is often not stated clearly. This may result in choosing a solution just because of its low cost, its ease of implementation, its lack of expected resistance, etc. However, these may not be good reasons or criteria for making the choice.

This pitfall is illustrated by the large car manufacturer who seemed to be obsessed with the cost effect of each design or engineering problem. The company's approach was simple—the least costly solution was the one that was chosen.

This approach completely ignored consumer safety, customer satisfaction, and product quality and durability. The result was that the company lost its market share to imports over the years.

They eventually adopted a new rationale for choosing between alternative solutions to these *(and other)* problems. The company agreed that each decision would consider the following criteria: customer satisfaction, safety, quality, durability, and cost.

By looking at all of these factors, the company began basing its design decisions on criteria that were important to the customer rather than just the cost consideration, which was not the right criterion to ensure long-term success.

PITFALL # 7

Failing To Plan Adequately How To Implement And Evaluate The Chosen Solution

A problem-solving team or individual can simply run out of energy at some point in the problem-solving process, and the important implementation and evaluation phases may not get the attention they deserve.

Implementation needs to be planned, managed, and monitored. The required resources need to be available and applied to the implementation of the solution. Otherwise, the groundwork up to this point would have been in vain.

A mid-size industrial equipment manufacturer had hired a consultant to spend a day working a special project team through a problem-solving session. They defined the problem, analyzed root causes, reviewed the data, brainstormed solutions, and agreed on two solutions to implement.

When the consultant checked back with the group a month later, she was surprised to discover that virtually nothing had been done.

As it turned out, the group had ended their session with the assumption that each of them knew what should be done and when. However, when they returned to their jobs, there were the usual fires to put out and issues to deal with, and each of them assumed the others were taking care of what had to be done to resolve the problem.

A subsequent session had to be called to develop a precise Action Plan, which outlined roles and responsibilities, time lines, resources, and desired outcomes. Then things started to happen. Without a plan nothing had happened, and nothing ever would have.

REFERENCE MATERIALS AND REPRODUCIBLE FORMS

BRAINSTORMING

Brainstorming is a technique to help you come up with several ideas. It's best to use in group problem-solving situations. It is a fast-moving process and it can be used to make a list of ideas at different stages of the problem-solving process.

How To Use Brainstorming

Brainstorming is a freethinking technique and it has some basic ground rules that make it effective. They are:

> ⇒ Avoid criticism and *"knocking down"* of ideas
>
> ⇒ Look for wild/exaggerated ideas
>
> ⇒ Go for quantity
>
> ⇒ Try to build on the ideas of others *(when in groups)*
>
> ⇒ Make a list *(to use later)*

The two most common Brainstorming methods are:

METHOD	THE WAY IT HAPPENS
Freewheeling	⇒ Share ideas all at once
	⇒ Make a list of the ideas as they are *"shouted out"*
Round robin	⇒ Everyone takes a turn and offers one idea
	⇒ Anyone can pass on any turn
	⇒ It continues until everyone has had a chance
	⇒ Make a list of all the ideas as they are offered

CAUSE AND EFFECT DIAGRAM

The Cause and Effect Diagram is a great tool for finding the *real* causes of a problem. If you use this technique, you will usually get a good definition of the problem.

Cause and Effect Diagrams are also called *"fishbones" (because of their shape)*. The visual nature of this method helps you to see patterns and relationships among causes.

How To Use Cause And Effect Analysis

❑ **Define the problem.**

Condense your problem statement to a few key words that describe the result or effect of the problem. Write this effect in a box on a large sheet of paper. For example, suppose the vending machine produces *"bad-tasting coffee"* all the time. Our first step on the Cause and Effect Diagram would look like:

| Bad-tasting |
| Coffee |

❑ **Define the major categories of causes of the problem.**

Look at the major categories of causes of the problem. The most popular categories are the 3-M's and a P: Machines, Methods, Materials, and People. These categories can be tailored to your specific problem-solving needs.

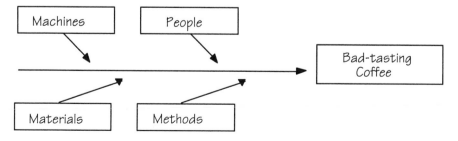

❑ **Brainstorm possible causes.**

Come up with as many ideas as you can for each category. For example, under machines, we note that the filter is broken.

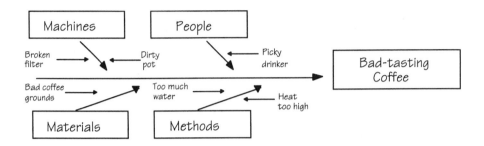

Sometimes one cause can build from another cause. For example:

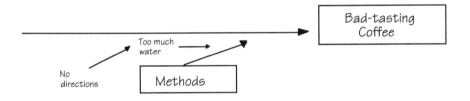

❑ **Identify the most likely causes.**

Avoid jumping to solutions such as, *"Buy a new coffeepot!"* while identifying possible causes. Look at all of the possible causes and narrow them down to the most likely causes. Use a reduction process or a tool such as Pareto analysis.

❑ **Make certain the most likely causes are real.**

This means you may have to gather more information.

CAUSE AND EFFECT WORKSHEET

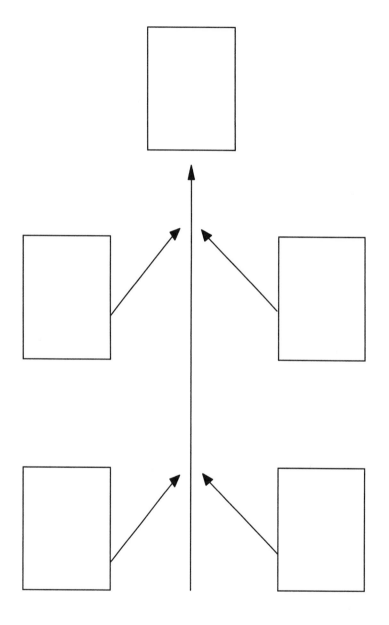

PARETO ANALYSIS

A Pareto Chart is a special type of bar graph that helps determine the relative frequency or importance of a number of different problems *(or causes)*. The bars are arranged in descending order, with the relatively important *(taller)* bars on the left and the less important *(shorter)* bars on the right.

How to Use Pareto Charts

Before constructing a Pareto Chart, it is recommended that you familiarize yourself with Check Sheets and other basic data-gathering techniques. *(These techniques are described in detail in two other publications in this series entitled Continuous Improvement Tools: Volume 1 and Volume 2.)*

Constructing a Pareto Chart consists of five major steps.

❏ **Identify the categories of problems *(or causes)* to be compared.**

(This can be obtained from a Cause and Effect Diagram, Brainstorming, Check Sheets, existing data, reports, etc.)

❏ **Select a standard unit of measurement and a time period to be studied.**

(Establish time parameters for data collection. Also determine the most useful unit of measurement for all categories.)

❏ **Collect and summarize data.**

➡ Use check sheets to collect data

➡ Obtain data from existing records

➡ Create a table for the data

Appropriate column titles should be identified *(i.e., category, frequency, percentages, etc.)*. Enter categories in descending order of frequency, with the most frequent at the top of the list. Also calculate percentages.

Example: Reasons why late to work *(80 days)*

Category	Frequency	% of Total	Cumulative
Traffic	30	38	38
Overslept	22	27	65
Late breakfast	12	15	80
Argue with spouse	11	14	94
Children	5	6	100
Total	80	100%	

❑ **Draw the horizontal and vertical axes.**

➠ Horizontal axis: Write in the categories on the axis in descending order, with the most frequently occurring category on the left.

➠ Left vertical axis: Write in the frequency on this axis. Scale it so that the value at the top of the axis is the sum of all occurrences.

➠ Right vertical axis: Write in the percent scale on this axis, with 100% at the top, opposite from the sum total on the left axis.

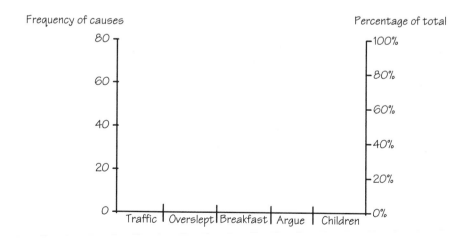

❏ **Plot bars on the Pareto Chart.**

Plot the data by constructing a series of bars in descending order of frequency.

Note: Categories with very few items can be combined into an *"Other"* or *"Miscellaneous"* category, which is placed on the extreme right as the last bar.

Label each axis and add a legend *(optional)*. The legend should contain the source of the data, who prepared it, date prepared, and any other relevant information.

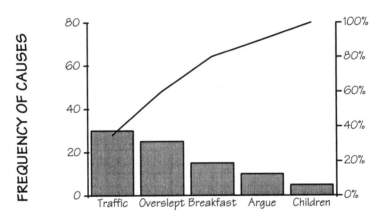

CAUSES FOR BEING LATE TO WORK

Cumulative line: to plot the cumulative line, place a dot above each bar at a height corresponding to the number on the percentage of total scale on the right vertical axis. Starting with the first column on the left, plot these dots from left to right, ending with the 100% point at the top of the right vertical axis.

PARETO CHART WORKSHEET

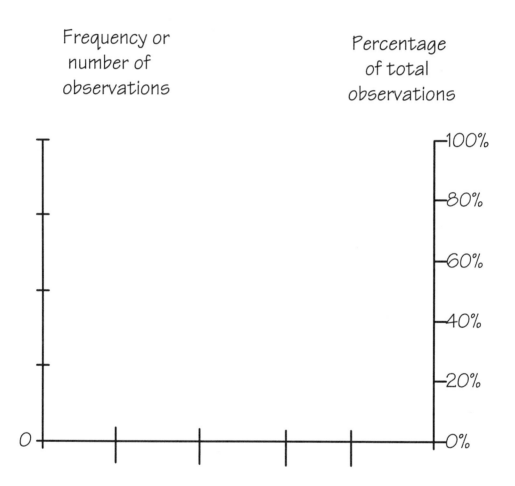

Frequency or
number of
observations

Percentage
of total
observations

100%

80%

60%

40%

20%

0

0%

CRITERIA RATING

The Criteria Rating technique lets you compare different solutions against a set of rules.

How To Use Criteria Rating

In buying a new home, for example, come up with your rules, or criteria, for making a decision (*e.g., location, cost, size, and design*). List these criteria on a sheet of paper and determine the appropriate *"weight"* for each item. Rate the three homes you are looking at against each criteria (*on a scale of 1 to 10*). Then multiply the rating by the weight to come up with a weighted score. Add up the weighted scores for each criterion and select the best alternative. **Note:** The *"weights"* should total 100%.

Home Example:

		RATING SCALE: 10 = High Preference 1 = Low Preference		
		ALTERNATIVES		
CRITERIA	**WEIGHT**	Home A	Home B	Home C
Location	40%	4 (1.6)	1 (.4)	3 (1.2)
Cost	30%	2 (.6)	4 (1.2)	3 (.9)
Size	20%	1 (.2)	2 (.4)	5 (1.0)
Design	10%	3 (.3)	4 (.4)	2 (.2)
TOTALS	100%	2.7	2.4	3.3
SUMMARY		Nice location; small	Great house; poor location	Large house; design so-so

ACTION PLANS

Action Plans let you communicate what needs to be done to put a solution into action. The Action Plan is an excellent tool for estimating what it will take to solve a problem. It helps you decide what to do first.

How To Use Action Plans

You can use an Action Plan to track steps or tasks. It can also be used to monitor the progress of a problem-solving solution. An Action Plan includes:

❑ **Action Step** *(A brief description of the step or task)*

Example: Write letter to all employees describing change in payroll system and cycle and the impact on paycheck of 2-7-91

❑ **Responsible Person** *(List of the person(s) who will be held accountable for achieving the Action Step)*

Example: B. Smith/Payroll-Author (primary) C. Fraser/HR-Reviewer E. Snyder/Office Services-Distributor

❑ **Begin Date/End Date** *(Start date and "drop dead" date)*

Example: 2-1-91/2-4-91

❑ **Estimated Hours** *(A "best guess" of the number of hours to complete a task)*

Example: 2

❑ **Cost** *(The amount of money needed to make it happen)*

Example: $70.00

❑ **Totals** *(Summary of what's needed to implement the plan)*

ACTION PLAN WORKSHEET

Action Step Task/Activity	Responsible Person/ Group	Begin Date	End Date	Estimated Hours	Cost
TOTALS					

THE PRACTICAL GUIDEBOOK SERIES
FROM RICHARD CHANG ASSOCIATES, INC.
PUBLICATIONS DIVISION

Our Practical Guidebook Collection is growing to meet the challenges of the ever-changing workplace of the 90's. Look for these and other titles from Richard Chang Associates, Inc. on your bookstore shelves and in book catalogues.

QUALITY IMPROVEMENT SERIES

Meetings That Work!

Continuous Improvement Tools Volume 1

Continuous Improvement Tools Volume 2

Step-By-Step Problem Solving

Satisfying Internal Customers First!

Continuous Process Improvement

Improving Through Benchmarking

Succeeding As A Self-Managed Team

MANAGEMENT SKILLS SERIES

Coaching Through Effective Feedback

Expanding Leadership Impact

Mastering Change Management

On-The-Job Orientation And Training

HIGH PERFORMANCE TEAM SERIES

Success Through Teamwork

Team Decision-Making Techniques

Measuring Team Performance

Building A Dynamic Team

ADDITIONAL RESOURCES
FROM RICHARD CHANG ASSOCIATES, INC.

Improve your training sessions and seminars with the ideal tools—videos from Richard Chang Associates, Inc. You and your team will easily relate to the portrayals of real-life workplace situations. You can apply our innovative techniques to your own situations for immediate results.

TRAINING VIDEOTAPES

Mastering Change Management
Turning Obstacles Into Opportunities*

Step-By-Step Problem Solving
A Practical Approach To Solving Problems On The Job*

Quality: You Don't Have To Be Sick To Get Better**
Individuals Do Make a Difference

*Authored by Dr. Richard Chang and produced by Double Vision Studios
**Produced by American Media Inc. in conjunction with Richard Chang Associates, Inc.
　Each video includes a Facilitator's Guide

"THE HUMAN EDGE SERIES" VIDEOTAPES***

Total Quality: Myths, Methods, Or Miracles
Featuring Drs. Ken Blanchard and Richard Chang

Empowering The Quality Effort
Featuring Drs. Ken Blanchard and Richard Chang

***Produced by Double Vision Studios

"THE TOTAL QUALITY SERIES"
TRAINING VIDEOTAPES AND WORKBOOKS

Building Commitment *(Telly Award Winner)*
How To Build Greater Commitment To Your TQ Efforts

Teaming Up
How To Successfully Participate On Quality-Improvement Teams

Applied Problem Solving
How To Solve Problems As An Individual Or On A Team

Self-Directed Evaluation
How To Establish Feedback Methods To Self-Monitor Improvements

Authored by Dr. Richard Chang and produced by Double Vision Studios, each videotape from *"The Total Quality Series"* includes a *Facilitator's Guide* and five (5) *Participant Workbooks* with each purchase. Additional *Participant Workbooks* available.

EVALUATION AND FEEDBACK FORM

In order to continuously improve the quality of the resources provided through Richard Chang Associates, Inc., Publications Division, we need your help. We would greatly appreciate your input and suggestions regarding this particular guidebook, as well as future guidebook interests.

Please photocopy this form before completing since other readers may use this guidebook. Thank you in advance for your feedback.

Guidebook Title: _____

1. Overall, how would you rate your *level of satisfaction* with this guidebook? Please circle your response.

   Extremely Dissatisfied   Satisfied   Extremely Satisfied

   1   2   3   4   5

2. What specific *concepts or methods* did you find <u>most</u> helpful?

   _____
   _____

3. What specific *concepts or methods* did you find <u>least</u> helpful?

   _____
   _____

4. As an individual who may purchase additional guidebooks in the future, what *characteristics/features/benefits* are most important to you in making a decision to purchase a guidebook *(or another similar book)*?

   _____
   _____

5. What additional *subject matter/topic areas* would you like to see available as a guidebook in the future?

   _____
   _____

Name *(optional):* _____

Address: _____

C/S/Z: _____ **Phone (   )** _____

PLEASE FAX YOUR RESPONSES TO: (714) 756-0853